Love, Lies and Lullabies

Copyright © 2018 **Ashley Jane**
Cover Art © 2018 **Nadiya Saara El-Sharkaway**

Ashley Jane - BreathWords
Alabama, USA
www.breathwords.com

All rights reserved. No part of this publication may be reproduced, distributed, or transmitted in any form or by any means, without prior written permission.

Author's Note: This is a work of fiction. Names, characters, places and incidents are a product of the author's imagination. Locales and public names are sometimes used for atmospheric purposes. Any resemblance to actual people, living or dead, or to businesses, companies, events, institutions, or locales are completely coincidental.

Love, Lies and Lullabies/Ashley Jane 1st Edition
ISBN 978-1-7325327-0-0

This book is dedicated to the lies that almost
break us, the love that tries to save us,
and the lullabies that remind us

there is poetry in our bones

Contents

Foreword — 5

Love — 9

Lies — 65

Lullabies — 119

Acknowledgements — 174

About the Author — 176

Foreword

Love, Lies and Lullabies tantalizes from the get-go with a title we all know too well, and it lures you in with its aesthetic appeal. This debut book of poetry and prose from **ASHLEY JANE**, *better known as "Breathwords" on many social media platforms* has been highly anticipated from fans all over the globe. With so many poetry books beckoning readers on social media today, Love, Lies and Lullabies *is a true standout.*

We are drawn to poetry because in its *condensed form*, it has the ability to levitate hearts and hydrate souls. When a writer scribes passages that let us *inhale and exhale* their pain, their past heartache, and their inner turmoil and never-ending strength... a reader will latch on and tangibly connect.

Prepare yourself. Ashley Jane's writing is addictive and infectious. You will find fragments of your *forgotten self* living inside her poems. You will think she is a mind reader or a magician, because the imagery she conjures in your head is pure magic. The depth of the way she conveys chapters like *Love, Lies and Lullabies*, are crafted with such skill, you will find yourself in awe at how easily her words mimic your own thoughts. *You feel freed. Understood. Comforted.*

This is a poetic book of empowerment, stemming from life experiences. Many of the writings shine light on overcoming toxic and painful relationships. The author's voice is fluent and eloquent. *Soothing, but not pacifying.* She understands pain. In creating this book, she is sharing her poetic lines with her readers, so they know *they are not alone in heartache.* I highly recommend Love, Lies and Lullabies, and I am thrilled to watch this new voice enter the publishing world.

Alfa

Author of *Abandoned Breaths, Silent Squall, Bouquets: Letting them Go, Monsoon, I find You in the Darkness, and Amid Thirsty Vines*

Love, Lies and Lullabies

We painted with words,
immortalized our souls with ink,
sold our hearts to the masses

Love

Ashley Jane

Love isn't perfection.
It isn't sunsets and rainbows.
It isn't declarations or words.
It's dedication.
It's loyalty and honesty.
It's battling through the bad times and enjoying the good.
It's acceptance of weaknesses and acknowledgment of strengths.
It's bravery and honor.
Love is unconditional, despite failures or mistakes.
It's understanding that there is no such thing as perfection.

(and still, love is everything)

For too long,
I was blind to my own needs,
searching for Mr. Perfect
and finding him in all the wrong places
and all the wrong faces
I pushed the boundaries
of what was good for me
while he waited
on the sidelines
letting me make
my own mistakes
(he always knew
I wasn't good at listening
when I didn't want to hear it)

All along,
what I was searching for
was right in front of me,
with softness
and whispers against my cheek

He has always been there
to listen
to hold
to love

(it just took time to open my eyes)

I was suffocating,
incapable of breathing
through all the silence
I was choking on every word
that went unsaid,
so many thoughts
bubbling at the surface,
waiting for someone, anyone

and when I found you,
it all came pouring out

Every breath
was a lifetime of words,
all previously unheard,
held in while I waited
for the right one
to hear them,
while I waited
for you

(this is what freedom feels like)

I could think all day
of all that love requires
If I lay here,
I could come up with a million reasons
that it won't work
But, I know us
I see the way you stare into my soul
We'll ride the thunder
through the storm

(we'll survive)

bits of bone
and broken hearts,
rough, uneven night

but, you are light,
pearl bright white

bringing love back
to forbidden places

(shimmer)

I remember the crash,
the quick descent,
the mighty shattering

a heart fragmented

but,
I also remember
his dark eyes
as he picked up
my ceramic heart,
all its pieces
put back together
by his careful hands

I guess that's
why they call it
falling in love

(*fragmented heart*)

We are designed
to escape the wreckage,
to hide from the phantoms and shadows,
to run when the world starts caving in
But, you build castles
from disasters
You color my world
with something new
and paint me in shades of home

(I am rebuilt with love)

He took the time
to meet my ghosts,
figured out my flaws,
danced with my darkness,

and his is still the only light
that scares my shadows away

(some light saves)

You and I,
we aren't put into one little box
We are rough and tumble,
soft and gentle,
dark and light,
the restless girl
and the kind-hearted boy
that loves all of her

(we are beyond definition)

You take away
my darkest nights,
my fractured parts
and broken heart
You hold me under velvet skies,
tracing each of my scars
and reminding me
that I am stronger
because of them,
leaving me enough of those shadows
to rebuild myself
with bits of love

(lesson in love)

Two independent threads
weft together,
creating a makeshift savior
by weaving my darkness into your light
I am stronger when bound to your touch
Your hands are the church steps leading to my salvation

(hallelujah, I am saved)

I let you in,
gave you permission
to burrow deep under my skin
And, you've left traces,
little whispers of yourself
in so many places
You crawled inside my soul
and made yourself a home

So, even when things aren't easy,
we will never be lost again

(the map lies within)

He is the lyrics
walking through my mind,

melody and magic
threaded together

by the notes of his words
and the music of his beating heart

(he is my favorite song)

We ushered in the spring,
days painted in blooming green,
nights spent sitting under a star studded sky
(I claimed the treasure in your eyes as mine)

Your lips tasted like pear and perfection,
and there were butterflies in your touch
I called you my perfect muse,
my precious lucky charm

...you still are

(I am the lucky one)

We spent the day
doing nothing,
and we found comfort
in knowing
that *nothing* was enough
We had no need
for fancy dates
and pretty flowers
It was just the two of us
celebrating another day together,
and neither of us needed
to make it anything more

(it's the simple things)

There is something delicate
in the way he holds my heart,
in the way he heals my weathered soul,
his fingers playing six strings across my skin

We are music

We are magic

We are love

(*delicate*)

Love, Lies and Lullabies

A voice reaches out,
little tendrils of sound
carried in the quiet
while eyes part at first light

shadows slide
as hands glide

and bodies move a little slower,
but with more fire
in their touch

(lost in this beautiful fire)

Ashley Jane

I love how
your words give you away
You keep trying to stay cool and collected,
but, I can hear your heart speed up,
and your breath is unsteady
every time we talk

(weak in the knees)

We meet between
stolen breaths
and crashing beats,
pulled into slow-spins
as night melds around us

We find redemption in soul stares
and healing in tentative touches

We never needed anything
to fill the silence

There is love in the quiet

(a perfect quiet)

Share your secrets
as you talk me to sleep
Whisper in my ear
all your pressing needs
Divulge your wants
Discuss your dreams
Tell me every
detail of every little thing
Convey your wishes
against my skin
Hold me close
and confess your sins
Reveal the demons
you try to hide away
Show me all the things
you're too scared to say
Admit. Confide. Disclose. Profess.
I want to know you
with every part of me

(I'm listening)

We wake
to sparks of fire
in shining eyes,

these flickering flames,
a heated reminder
that chases away
the midwinter chill

(we soak up the warmth)

Ashley Jane

I read you like a book,
engrossed in every chapter
I soak up every page,
hooked from beginning to

                                            end

(I read it over and over)

I found you somewhere
in a sea of passing moments
We danced in greetings,
and goodbyes became lost
in whispers and glances
and good morning kisses

I made your soul my sanctuary
I turned your heart into my home

(your arms are my abode)

Part these walls
where my truth lies hidden
Let my soul spill open,
a slow drift towards home
We are crashing nights
and free falling days
but, your hands are my rope,
and I am no longer afraid of falling

(you chase the fear away)

intimacy in silence,
quietly, you cleanse the dirt from my soul

I let your fingers
trace the poetry in my veins,
felt your insatiable hunger
for a taste of my words

I found absolution in this happiness,
your hands holding my dreams
your pulse beating with my own

(I found my home)

I can taste the way poetry whispers
within each kiss,
passion and destiny colliding in this
dancing stardust wonder,

love and magic living fearlessly
on your parted lips

You know just how to breathe me in
You know just how
to bring me to life

(we are the wonder)

I am soul words
seen by his hopeful eyes,
quiet moments
seeking a sweet life,
watching him in sacred silence
as emotions bloom across his face,
the quick beat of my poet's heart
held in his care and kissed by grace

(grace tastes like him)

You made a home in my lungs,
your touch forever blooming
in caves and chambers
I'd once closed off
You bloom in my darkness,
each petaled promise
giving me a beautiful reason
to breathe

(each inhale is filled with you)

I love finding you
in every letter that I pen,
in the hidden moments
where I worship
your name on the page
and praise the words that emerge
to carry me through
You stole the worries
that haunted my heavy heart,
then fed them back to me as poetry
that my greedy soul devoured

(I call you praise poetry)

Home is
twisted up in his origami heart
with its shimmering shine,

(people write love songs
about the way he creates art)

and I remain
entranced by eyes
that never stray
while his every word
falls upon me,
stripping past
all layers of pretense

He watches me unwaveringly
as my heart lies bare,
waiting to be discovered
and twisted up in his

(yeah, it is that kind of love)

Deeper I fall,
down the slope of hard lines,
tangled up in twisting vines

I suppose the flowers
within me
bloom best
buried in the shadows
of his cimmerian heart

(cimmerian heart)

Comfort exists
in the sound of your voice
Heaven lingers
in your soft touch
Home is found
in your dark eyes,
and I never want to leave

(I am staying)

I know I lean on you
to hold me
more than I should
I know that I am
strong enough to stand alone

But, some days,
it's nice to know
that I don't have to hold myself up,
that I can call on you,
that it's ok to call your shoulder
home

(thank you for that)

Ashley Jane

I love how you listen
to the way my heart beats
as you hold me close,
the way it calls out to you
in a language
only you can understand
It speaks in tongues,
in a stutter start pulse
But, you always know just how
to decipher every word

(*this is our private language*)

I am rough cut, wild
with an erratic pulse
and a tendency to run
Yet, you hold me still
with a look
with a whisper
Your heart beats steadfast,
and you remain
polished, controlled, focused
My nerves are raw
My mind is tired
My bones ache
But, your name is on my lips,
and your kiss
offers salvation

Your hands feel like the only shelter
that will stand through my storm

(I am safely contained within your walls)

I scratched my name
into your skin,
and you called yourself
    MINE

There are too many moments
where I am losing focus,
where the world tilts off its axis,
and I am losing control
    YOU CALLED YOURSELF MINE

You reel me in
with whispers of truth
There is sanity in your touch
and hope in your eyes
    I CALL YOU MINE

My mind can finally breathe
when you call my name
    I AM YOURS, TOO

(mine)

He paints me whole,
filling in the spaces,
creating a portrait
of the woman within,
capturing the true soul
that flows under my skin,
incorporating all
the scars and marks,
removing the scratches
that would do me harm,
coloring the stains
that came with time,
repairing the cracks
that were left behind
He sees me,
sees past the flaws
He paints me whole again

(I become whole with him)

Ashley Jane

Too many things get mistaken for love
because people think love doesn't make demands
It does (oh, how it does)

Love is not all gentle days and softness
It is reckless
It hurts
It burns deep within your veins

It is easy to fake
        the good things,
        the pretty things,
        the safe things

but,
love is not always good
        and pretty
        and safe

It is messy and chaotic,
and we get tangled up in it
We fall madly into it
We get lost in it
We live for it
We try to define it,
but it is not meant to be defined

Love, Lies and Lullabies

We think we can create it
by planting gardens
and waiting for them to blossom
on sunny days
But, what we fail to realize
is that love is not roses

Love is a forest
filled with wildflowers
that only bloom
on dark nights

(love is messy)

Ashley Jane

You hold both my hand
and my heart,
keeping me close
even when I push you away,

and I know that I do push you away

But, you stay,
always by my side,
reminding me of who I am
even when I forget
or try to make myself
into something else

You say my name
like it's your favorite word,
and I know that we are real,
that we are constant,
a promise,
a big bang love
that ties your heart to mine

(the only constant)

I like the way
your eyes begged me to stay,
even as your lips whispered goodbye,
the way you came back for one last kiss
(Neither of us was very good at leaving)

I like the way
you laugh as I dare you
to escape the rules,
to color outside the lines
(Your smile remains my favorite sight)

I like the way
you watch me when I'm deep in thought,
ink rushing across the page,
trying to capture every moment
(Staying was the best decision I ever made)

(staying was the thing that saved me)

Ashley Jane

You are the storm
behind my words,
the race of thoughts
stampeding in my head,
demanding release,
the poetic tempest
pouring out in
ink-stained torrents,
unbridled, unconfined
You are the strength
that keeps me going,
and I need you more
than you could
ever know

(*you are always my strength*)

You are a song
heard all around,
found by accident
and sung on
gray mornings
and late
November nights
as we sit under the stars
and watch the
box cars go by,
admiring the graffiti
and reminding
ourselves that
everything doesn't
have to be so
damn complicated

(the perfect reminder)

I held on to the magic
of vibrant gray storms
and pretty jeweled skies,
both a stirring, soul sight

I clung to hope
through the murky days
when color would fade,

to the timeless nights
beneath star light

I embraced
the here and now,
with you,
with us,

because, we are infinite,

and I always knew
that together, we'd fly

(*we will always fly*)

I don't say it enough,
those little words,
thanking you
for holding me together,
for letting me be honest
when my mind wants to run

I watch how you give all you can,
putting your heart and soul
into each brush of your hand

Your touch promises to see us through

We are two halves of a whole
making memories in magic moments

(we will make it)

Ashley Jane

I always called myself a winter soul,
but you made me love
the way the air felt crisp
while the leaves painted the ground
in autumn hues
Your face still lights up most
when they start to change

We used to drive for hours to pick apples
and harvest pumpkins
We would revel in the beauty
of the Shenandoah Valley,
soaking up nature
and finding out of the way places

We explored little towns
on the edge of nowhere,
created our own little mini-adventures
(Do you remember how we would drive an hour
just to get groceries? It was mainly an excuse
to leave the city. I let you drag me into
comic book stores just to see
how excited it made you)

We made Williamsburg our place,
visiting every Thanksgiving
and many times in-between
The people in the little shops knew our name,
and that was ok with us

We sought out eclectic shops
and weird museums,
and we made so many memories

I know it is not the same now
This place is smaller,
and there is far less to do here

I know we both miss the adventures

But, I think it was never about the towns
or the shops or museums

It was about us
losing ourselves in the quiet moments
away from everyone and everything

Let's lose ourselves again

(cheers to new adventures)

Ashley Jane

I sometimes bottle things up,
pretend it's okay

I leave feelings unclaimed
because I always thought it was better that way
(they try, but people don't always understand)

but, here you are, offering more,
shouldering the bad day,
the pulse of pain
that lurks deep within
(you make my scarlet heart
want to beat again)

so I breathe you in

people move mountains,
over the sound of a kiss
and soul searching eyes

you bring me home with yours

 (home is in your heart)

I let you get lost
in my forest of haunting nightmares,
(only heartache knows
how to grow in this darkness)

I let you cut yourself on all my broken pieces
as they fell in a wave of loss and leaves

But, you turned my soul screams
into soft woodnote melodies

You took the time
to teach the flowers how to bloom
(I'll forever be grateful for you)

(you saw the promise of petals)

I bound us in eternities,
two anxious hearts forever linked

We are equal measure give and take,
warm arms that hold and soothe the ache
of our breakable souls,
our delicate smiles more tenuous than most

We cling to us, to this
because it's what love is

(we are love)

I watched in awe,
the way you wove lights together,
stringing my weaknesses and strengths,
your stardust magic creating new constellations

You painted shimmer into shadow,
blended my wild heart with the precious peace
that lingered under your skin,
and I fell in love
with your galaxy view

You made the night
beautiful

(I danced in your stardust magic)

There are lines from poems
that steal my breath,
that make me stand still and soak them in,
a lot like people do sometimes,
like you do
when you say something unexpected
or whisper something sweet
or call my name like it is water
and you are dying of thirst

Yeats wrote The Second Coming,
visions of a land post-war,
a beast looming towards
a world that stands on the edge of anarchy,
veering too close to an apocalypse
that will end in destruction
He says, "Things fall apart;
the centre cannot hold"

But, I think Yeats forgets
that we house
the most powerful tool
in our chests,
something that will
withstand the catastrophe
and bind us together
even when the world
is barely hanging on

Love, Lies and Lullabies

I think he forgets
that love is madness
and miracle,
and it too steals your breath

you and I,
we hold its magic

and I know that the center will hold,
because we are the center,
and the circle around us is unending

(remember, we are the center)

Ashley Jane

Lies

I remember
the moment I lost you,
convincing myself it was something I did

And, I remember
the moment I realized
that our collapse wasn't my fault
It wasn't yours either really

See, you never learned how to tell the truth,
and I knew that,
but believed you anyway

(the lies we believe)

We are taught by movies
to love with abandon,
to throw caution to the wind
and run head first into the storm

We fall for the fantasy
and try to make it a reality,
but real love isn't picture perfect,
and it took me far too long
to stop falling for actors
who use hearts for a stage

(Romeo isn't real)

I spill a lot of words
about relationships

love
lust
longing
lies

(Those L words really get me,
        especially that last one)

I've got a knack
for picking liars out from a crowd,
    that back booth bar room brooder
    with a smile that kills
    and eyes you want to fall into

They always know just the right words
to pull me a little off center
Then, they swoop in with their charm,
acting like they know
just how to put all my pieces back together,
pieces that were broken
long before they came around,
pieces that will only shatter more
before they leave

(the L words)

Words dangling,
   run-on sentences
   jammed together
because talking is pointless
when no one listens,
and listening is pointless
when everyone lies

(this whole mess is pointless)

We were like glass,
fragile and delicate
and too easily broken
into heart-piercing shards

I tried to fix us,
tried to reassemble the pieces,
using light to cut out the dark
as if I could work Kintsugi magic
and repair all the pain with gold
But, the cracks had reached the soul

(I think,
sometimes,
we have to let them grow,
sever the bad to save the whole)

So, we shattered,
and I let the pieces fall where they may
because,
I knew I'd never be able to find them all,
much less reassemble them anyway

(we remain scattered pieces)

I wasted too much time
spilling my soul to a shadow
that chose to hear the masses
rather than the voice on his shoulder,
rather than the heart in his hands

I wasted too much energy
listening to the cries for attention,
offering up support to the stranger
who pretended we were friends

(it's the ones you think you know)

We were always good at pretending,
convincing ourselves
that the path we were on was straight,
lying to ourselves to avoid taking the blame

We were masters of deception,
foolishly so,
spending far too much time learning
how to be experts at pushing people away,
especially the ones that we wanted
(needed)
to stay

(just call us pretenders)

Tell me again
how it wasn't pretend
I love watching you
squirm as you lie

(pass the popcorn)

I always took comfort
in the words you spilled
at 4am
It was in those wee hours
right before the sun lit the sky
that you were most honest

(4am is the hour of truth)

I inhaled
every word you said,
and now
I'm struggling
to breathe through
all the lies of yours
I swallowed

(suffocating)

I listened
to the way pretty fallacies
rolled off your tongue
You were such a master
of honey-coated lies,
your pathological lips
spilling venom in disguise,
firing words without warning
and pretending it's okay
You were darkness dressed up,
all bullets and bouquets

(shotgun liar)

Your words
infiltrate,
clawing their way
beneath my skin,
and I'm trying
to rip them out
before they become
another scar
that I have to hold onto

(claw marks)

Brittle bones
threaded together
Fragile cage
torn apart
Holder of secrets,
broken open,
granting access
to her heart
So frail
and delicate,
crumbling under
your hand's touch
holding on to
a tenuous hope
that it won't
break too much

But, it always does

(some things are made to be broken)

Secrets,
weathered and worn,
treacherous truths
hidden within
your saccharine kisses
and lying eyes,
the devil inside
now magnified,
an undeniable creed
of dishonest greed
And me,
back turned,
too naive
to see
the renegade beneath
your bewitching allure

(the devil always has secrets)

He beckons
with flowers
and false promises,
tempting you
to sell your soul

He invites you into bed
with deception,
tries to seduce you with lies,
bargaining your freedom
for a little piece of happiness

(your soul is not for sale)

I watched her
while she waited for your return,
past the point when most would have given up,
when they would have walked away

She stayed,
and she waited,
and I held her hand knowing that
you would probably break her heart

She patiently gave you all the time and space
that you never said you needed

She waited for you,
and you couldn't even give her
the decency
of saying goodbye

Your lies never deserved her hello

(she was too good for you)

She plucks another
from his pack of lies,
fingers fumbling with each word
as she lights it up,
taking a long drag of every letter
and letting them sink into her system,
too addicted to their burn
to ever give up the habit

(chainsmoker)

You were always excellent
at running away,
at placing blame,
at shifting the focus
from your own mistakes

You were an expert
at making sure
you came out looking clean

But, I still see the dirt underneath

(there are smudges under the surface)

Your entire aura
is simply serpentine,
slyness oozing from every pore,
darkness at your very core
You camouflage it in pretty shades,
wanting us on edge,
so smart and devious
that you practically slither
You call it coy or mischievous,
but, I call it downright
sinister

(snake in the grass)

You never thought twice,
deftly handing me your heart of ice,
having me place it
near the fire of my own

but, your type of cold
can never be thawed,

and you left mine bitten
with an unwavering frost

I don't know if I'll ever get warm

(your type of cold is bitter)

I was tricked
by the king of crows,
his cobalt heart brimming
with a world rimmed in ice
I dipped my soul
into pools of cerulean,
fooled by their luminous shine
I tasted a kiss of falling petals
from arctic lips full of lies,
but, I'll no longer
fall for the half-truths
of moody blue valentines

(I never liked the blues)

I graced you
with a rain of roses
and crown of lilies,
loved you like autumn
with a touch of spring
I fed you euphoria
and rainbow dreams,
but, nothing is as it seems

You were delusion
wrapped up in lies,
danger wrapped up in
soft petals that hide

Now, I won't be swayed
by pretty things

I see the thorns in your veins

(you can dress it up, but it's still a lie)

I fell head first
into the trap you set
I let you in,
your bullets and bullshit spinning under my skin

I felt you crashing your way through my veins,
a treacherous curse of my own making
because I failed to see
that you were ruthless and reckless

I found no leniency in your fingertips,
no blessings to be counted in your touch

You were waves of war disguised as love,
but I wasn't prepared for battle

(pulled under by waves of war)

Your words
echo in the halls,
reverberating on bathroom walls,
and I am screaming profanities
to the night...

(Damn, woman, be strong)
   ...but I am barely hanging on

These rooms
have become hotel tombs,
and I've laid you to rest,
but there is no drug strong enough
to rid me of these
haunting memories

 (I'm buried in memories)

We were nothing more
than truths
extinguished
by the sound of the wind,
promises swept away
when daylight began to fade,
a sudden change of heart
following after the dark

and now, nothing will be the same

(how the winds change)

I tried
bridging the shores,
tried plotting our course,
two different souls
going wherever the wind blows

but my survival was tied
to a sinking ship,
your bloodthirsty words
leaving my defenses
slashed to ribbons

So, I learned
that some structures are made
to come tumbling down,

all that was left
now floating with death

I guess some hearts were made to drown

(going down with the ship)

I hung your farewells
on the rack by the door,
a reminder that all of your
half-hearted hellos
eventually led to goodbyes

(au revoir)

You were a shot of whiskey
blazing straight to my core,
the fire and the sting,
a fabricated bliss
racing through the veins,
bringing a high that never lasts
and a hell of a crash
as it wore off at 3am,
leaving me numb
in the worst way,
desperately trying to scrub myself clean,
praying for absolution,
promising
that you were a mistake
I'd never make again

But, I was always a glutton for punishment,
and I desperately craved the burn

(the burn beckons)

I drank it all in,
absinthe lies
on ice,
and me, chasing an emotional high

I let you seep into my veins,
thinking you were the breaker of chains
I gave you my pain,
a black china melody
with a
shattering
refrain

Now, I'm purging
your name,
each letter shot,
bullet wound exits
in an explosion
of thought

(call me a casualty)

Ashley Jane

You hung up
pretty words,
but, your heart is still a prison

You held me captive in it

(in captivity)

I made you a mix tape,
black, like my heart,
filled with songs of how I'm always wrong
                    (and you never are)

I hope you feel every beat
Let the pulse thrum through you
while the words sink in,
reminding you of all the things
that you'll miss,
all the things you'll never find again

(this one is for your mix tape)

You preferred
to dress up in pretty lies
and charades,
but I wasn't made like you

Give me honesty
and ugly truths

(I'm too old for dress up)

You know who you are,
you who lurks in shadows
waiting for the perfect moment to act,
you who is quick to judge and quicker to attack

You linger
between the lines
of poems past done
You push and break
until insisting you've won

There is no compassion
in your heart

The shelves are empty, and the rooms are dark
And, while it still beats,
there is no soothing melody,
only an eerie quiet exists,
echoing in each chamber with emptiness

(empty hearts can't sing)

I met you for a rendezvous
under a silver sky moon,
felt the sting of your piercing high
I fell for the darkness in your eyes
(You filled my veins with fire and lies)
But, I am more
than the broken spirit
and crushed-daisy heart
you tried to leave me with,
and I've learned
how to breathe through the ache

(a letter to past demons)

You wove your words into my skin,
planted them like roses to bloom
and I felt them blossom,
bringing thorns with them
You hid the pain in prettiness
as those thorns cut deep,
slicing open my veins,
filling me with your hostility
and that carefully disguised rage
I'm still not the same
where you wounded my heart
I wear scars
I hate roses
And, you remain
unforgiven

(these wounds won't heal)

I was the outsider,
summoned by the hum
in your veins,
disappearing into
the shadows you'd create

Your hands were always best
at shifting stars,
folding them
and moulding them
into something dark

I guess I was just another origami heart

(tenebrific)

We fooled ourselves,
became blinded
by the illusion
Our bulletproof lies
really weren't
all that bulletproof

And, now we're
a little less together,
a little too numb
to fully wrap
our minds around
how the holes in our hearts
are where the bridges were
before they came crashing down

(bullets brought down the bridges)

I sipped slow
on your elixir of pretty words,
let them melt like candy
on my tongue,
bombarded with the pleasure
of your warmth,
your sun-kissed seduction,
swayed by your charm
and flooded
with your flattery
(overwhelmed,
just how you wanted me to be)

But, the heat
soon turned to ice,
and I stood there frozen,
your claws digging deep
while you reveled in
a derailing destruction,
the old pleasure vanishing
within my puzzle box heart,
buttoned up and locked
(though you certainly tried
to tear it apart)

Now,
I've re-stitched it together
with sweetgrass and sage,
made it stronger,
cleansed the air of your name,
an allegory of faith
and a story of strength
held firmly in its chamber walls

(love bombed)

I stood on the shore
of bitterness,
let myself get lost in
waves of rage

but, I no longer wish to dwell
on hurt and hate and jealousy

I'll push those thoughts out to sea,
and ride the tides that change overnight,
sweeping water and words
under the bridge
as I coast on through
without the smallest thought of you

(I call this ocean 'apathy')

I can feel them lurking
in the back of my throat,
moments and mistakes
that my mind won't let go,
hovering there,
ensuring I don't forget,
turning them into lessons
of anger and regret
that I was naive enough
to allow myself
to be changed
into someone else,
and you stand there watching
as I fight each reminder
But I will not keep you there

I will build my walls taller
to keep you away
and any lingering memories
that want to stay
as I continue to try
to right all these wrongs,
embracing the happiness
that was here all along

(you've been locked out)

I suppose I believed
that you were the glue
holding my pieces together

You certainly pretended to be,
binding yourself to my every thought

Turns out,
they don't crumble
without you after all

(no adhesive necessary)

I found silence again,
your voice no longer haunting
all my sleepless nights
I found strength again,
in conversations with myself,
in moving on from everything else

Your words were sticks and stones,
my heart barely sheltered
behind fragile bones

But, I healed the bruises
that you left behind
I found hope
in the quiet

(sticks and stones didn't break me)

I got tired
of daisies and butterflies,
of this heartbreak fever burning under my skin

I got tired of delicate roses that wilt,
of your vines of love that were more like weeds

I bloom for myself now,
strong like forgotten snow pansies
pushing up from beneath the frost,
like wild honeysuckle climbing high

I thrive now
        because I am no longer rooted in you

(re-potted heart)

Everything with you
was black and white,
right and wrong,
bad and good
Nothing was ever debatable
Nothing was in-between

You could only see things
in your own light,
and you never tried
to understand mine

And all at once,
it came rushing to me
I am everything
you would never be,
and you are everything
I never want to become

(we will never be the same)

I taught myself
to filter through the fallacies,
to look beneath
the silent words buried deep

I learned
to unearth the hidden meanings,
to see the truth in the lie

Then, I figured out how to say goodbye

(self-taught)

I kept their names
(scrawled with disdain)
tucked away in a little black book
where I wouldn't look
I relegated them to unread pages,
the pretty liars with a bitter taste,
the chased muses
no longer worth the chase
Then, I locked it up safe
and tossed the key

(but first, I added your name)

It was always you,
the haunting thoughts
of something you said,
the persistence of a memory
that lingered behind,
the way it worked its way inside,
like a dangerous passenger
of a vulnerable mind
and an innocent heart

See, I let your words tear me to pieces,
painful lies presented like terrible truths
but, it doesn't end here
and I don't belong to you

(this is the beginning of your end)

I refuse
to lose myself
in your version
of truth

(some facts are simple)

I got your call,
your emails,
your messages,
all asking for forgiveness

but, you must have forgotten
that you were the one
who told me I was weak
because I was too forgiving

(I'm not weak anymore)

It was never enough,
the way I bent myself
to fit your mould,
destined to feel your morning chill
instead of the warmth that I deserved

I lingered too long
in your storm surge
of vicious words,
instead of breaking
the bridges apart,
escaping your reign
of hurt and hate,
refusing to die from
a broken heart

And, only time will tell
how well I'll heal,
but it's finally time to start

(we call it a healing process)

Ashley Jane

Love, Lies and Lullabies

Lullabies

Ashley Jane

He lingers in the silence,
weaving through
our words,
our actions,
our choices,
always present and watching
as we wish for more of him,
or hope that he passes faster

He is neither friend, nor enemy,
just a gentle reminder that,
sometimes, we need to move on

(time waits for no one)

I was never
really that good
at holding onto hope,

preferring to dwell
in the land of bitter reality

But, deep inside,
I think I was meant
to be a believer,
sheltered by trees
and guided by stars

(one day, I'll believe)

I wrote down
all those 3am thoughts,
kept them tucked away in a safe place,
all those sad pleas from a broken soul
and the angry words of a blackened heart

But, I got tired of remembering,
of being pulled back into the dark

And, as I watched the sun start to fade away
I fed my words to the waves
and watched them get pulled out to sea

(now the ocean reads my poetry)

Talk to me
in a bluer shade,
like the indigo
that colors the sky
each night
or the ocean's turquoise
sent to carry me away

(let me dream in blues)

Slip me something
so I can slip into slumber,
where liquid pictures
pulse through my veins,
a rush caused
by sweet Morpheus
creating dreams

(sleep is a drug)

Tell me a story
before I fall asleep

one of a rose-tinted world
where I don't find myself
                constantly
                  falling

one of magic and mystery,
of truth laced with fantasy

Fold it up for me,
a pocket-size, portable paradise
for every time I close my eyes

I need a little peace
before I sleep

(bedtime story)

We are
the broken ones,
the ones who feel it all,
the ones who
want to make it better

We cling to each other
because we recognize
the pain

(like souls)

Time flies,
adrift in the wren's
wandering heart

floating in
the simple truths
of a blackbird's
soulful song

(time moves on the wind)

We dug deep beneath the cracks
and found ourselves below the surface
We traded melancholy for meaning,
swapped cowardice for courage
We exchanged lies for love
and discovered promise
blooming beneath shimmering stars

We learned how to shine bright too

(metanoia)

Some days,
she still gets lost
in a lonely forest filled with lullabies,
busily chasing down secrets
in fading photographs
and listening for answers in the wind's song

She is a feather
f
 a
  l
   l
    i
     n
      g
amidst the leaves,
a soft soul quietly searching for strength

(she will find herself one day)

I think our hearts
become graveyards
for shooting stars,
and that we bury them
close to the surface,
watching over them
just in case
the wishes we made
still have a chance
at coming true

(we mark them with flowers)

Ashley Jane

We are bones
left in a state of disrepair,
held together
with threads of words
and moments of hope

(hope holds us together)

I am doubt found
in hidden corners,
moody blues and a closet filled with fear
But, you are made of hope,
40 million rainbows and a marigold sky,
lilac rivers running through your veins
and sunlight in your eyes

You fly with faith, bold butterfly

(please, never stop dreaming)

Ashley Jane

Coolness against warm skin,
these silver storms that wash the day away,
absolution found in the cleansing rain
that breathes me in and eases the ache

I make wishes on each falling drop

(let's dance in the rain)

Memories & mementos
of first glances & second chances,
photos of happy faces
and favorite places,
bits & pieces
of distant dreams,
stored away for recollection,
all these things,
material things,
with moments tied to them,
begging for a trip down memory lane

But, I'd rather focus
on your words etched into my mind,
scored into my bones,
the way you reach out to my soul,
your calmly whispered song
that keeps me whole,
the reminders that will not fade,

words that no one can steal away

(you are the poem I read before bed)

Ashley Jane

We are dreamers,
the hum of the night
running through our veins,
speaking to us in the language of shooting stars,
in the dialect of shadows that ripple and move,
in bits of glimmering light

We believe in star-fire and moon-magic,
enchanted by the way they fuel our hearts
and save our souls

We are the ones the night calls
when she is lonely for company

(the night is made for dreamers)

Our place
was where water met wind,
summer days by the lake,
sunlight and loud music
and confessions beneath the stars

So many years later,
we still think of this as home

(this will always be home)

Ashley Jane

We keep listening
to windy hymns beneath blue skies,
let the calm chase away the madness
when anxiety hits a bit too hard

We trade the yellow sun day for the alpenglow,
our souls in sync with the horizon,
patiently waiting until our hearts
can spill secrets to the dark

(remember, the stars are always listening)

There is something true about the sun,
something honest in the way it rises and sets,
as if it knows we need a little light to guide us,
but also understands that we're a little dark too

I remember in college,
on those early mornings
after nights I couldn't sleep
I'd sit on the balcony
watching the leaves change color
They always seemed so vibrant in the dawn's glow

And, in grad school, that night I sat beside you
taking in the city skyline as the day faded,
orange and pink skies drinking in the moonlight
until only the star-studded black remained

There is a certain peace in knowing
that I'm never watching it alone,
Somewhere, someone else is captivated,
soul bound to the sky
and the sun

(Namaste)

Ashley Jane

We pause,
a split-second glimpse,
afraid we might miss it,
this secret universe around us

We dare to dance
in the stories of someone else,
chaotically chasing telescopic moments in time,
a journey in the blink of an eye

(we are mere specks in the sonder)

There is something true about the sun,
something honest in the way it rises and sets,
as if it knows we need a little light to guide us,
but also understands that we're a little dark too

I remember in college,
on those early mornings
after nights I couldn't sleep
I'd sit on the balcony
watching the leaves change color
They always seemed so vibrant in the dawn's glow

And, in grad school, that night I sat beside you
taking in the city skyline as the day faded,
orange and pink skies drinking in the moonlight
until only the star-studded black remained

There is a certain peace in knowing
that I'm never watching it alone,
Somewhere, someone else is captivated,
soul bound to the sky
and the sun

(Namaste)

We pause,
a split-second glimpse,
afraid we might miss it,
this secret universe around us

We dare to dance
in the stories of someone else,
chaotically chasing telescopic moments in time,
a journey in the blink of an eye

(we are mere specks in the sonder)

daisy-chain crowns
and a soul rising sun on the horizon
It sets softly behind a blanket of clouds
until night's dream sings of sweet peace,
our heart scars kissed by stars
so that we may sleep
serene

(lulled by night)

a universe
of solitary moments
that defy meaning,
bound into perfect pieces,
creating a home
for lost souls to belong

(you asked me to define art)

I let the wind tell me stories
of beginnings,
a prologue written
on soft shoulders,
spilled ink
creating stories that
trail across my skin
It recites tales
of paper towns
too difficult to find,
only mapped with words
that follow my veins,
I feel it read
the psalms and promises
etched into my palms,
slow-breeze fingertips
tracing honest truths
in the outline
of my heart

(the day nature read me aloud)

These nights are spent
wrapped in the arms of the moon,
its soft blush touch against rose gold skin
slowly waking the wild within

She comes alive under purple midnight skies
while elusive magic floats through the breeze,
seducing the chaos in her veins
and setting it ablaze

(the moon sings of magic)

She builds a home
on breath and bones,
under a moon's glow,
in a nest of dreams
amidst the trees
that softly sway
like strong arms,
holding her steady
while soothing
her soul

She is floating on leaves
made of words,
wrapped up in
a blanket of stories
and songs and poems,
of memories that
feed her mind
and remind her to live

(home is where the moon is)

Ashley Jane

She is the bridge
between art and pain,
the silent pause
that becomes caught
in the wind and waves,
a whisper of mortality
that is hard to describe,
ephemeral and transient,
so beautifully tragic
as she rambles along
going nowhere and anywhere,
becoming lost in thought,
wavering in your mind
as she searches for
some unknown destination
that will never exist,
that cannot be defined,
drawn by some
cosmic connection,
some unrelenting need
to turn your tears into poetry,
words that sing on the page,
a slow melodic lullaby,
a beautifully, immortalized ache

(*she makes for gorgeous poetry*)

We plant hope
beneath the window
to ward away the darkness
We grow peace
like lilies
to stand sentry by the door

(flower guards)

Ashley Jane

She is a ripple in the ocean,
a barefoot gypsy with a sea glass heart
She dreams in the spring breeze,
chases the misty morning sunshine
until it fades late in the day
She paints the sky with streamers
of depth and dark and crystalline stars

(I call her Mother Nature)

Seeking honesty
beside the ocean

Chasing sincerity
through the trees

for nothing is truer
than words of waves
and falling leaves

(nature is filled with truth)

Falling words
floating down,
nature's way of whispering
sweet nothings
while undisclosed secrets
sweep through the trees
spilling mysteries
in hushed tones,
telling of places unexplored
and knowledge unrevealed

(there are secrets in these woods)

Let's turn it all off,
the lights,
the day,
the anxiety coursing through our veins

We are more than tired eyes
and unsteady hearts

Let's turn it all off
and watch the stars

(a penny for some peace and quiet)

Ashley Jane

It is the way the music plays
and matches my mood
and the beauty
surrounding everything:
people, places, nature

It is the brush of a touch
against bare skin,
the depth of knowledge
found in the eyes,
the whisper of a voice
that speaks to the soul

But, most of all,
the deeper meanings
and hidden emotions
that all this creates,
too often kept buried,
and in desperate
need of release

(you asked me to define poetry)

We stand under gemstone skies
with a palm full of sunlight
and constellations in our souls,
a myriad of moments woven
within the silence,
galaxies of distant dreams and memories

We are malleable madness
and magic,
whispers that hint
of another world beyond the stars,
a universe where this
(every tiny, minute, indescribable molecule)
was all worth saving

(hope for humanity)

We shine
through the darkness,
bold and bright,
even on those days
where everything seems
impossible
We shine
through the moments
where it seems
we might crumble
and fall apart
We shine
because there is no fault
in our stars,
only hope
and life
and love

(we shine because we must)

We are free spirits,
lost in the music
as we savor the sound

We are the stars falling down
as the sun begins to rise,
the touch of color
staining midnight skies

We are dream catchers
caught by the moonlight
a tangled twist of gypsy magic,
the touch of
the everlasting,
an aeonian grace that shines

(we are equal parts day and night)

Ashley Jane

We wove mystery
and melancholy,
dovetails
and daydreams,
got lost in the mountains,
found ourselves
by the sea
We made love to the moon,
let the dawn be our muse,
our hearts tethered
to their magical glow,
in love with all the secrets they hold,
the brilliant mystique
just out of reach
of our wanderlust souls
We chased after something
we didn't know,
the shine,
the thrill,
that certain something
we just had to
feel

(*we wrote songs of our adventures*)

I believe
in moments
filled with madness,
in emotions
that stir the inner fire,
in the way your light
fills the room

(I believe in simple magic)

It is those moments
when I feel outside myself,
those vivid moments under gray skies
where I stand there with open eyes,
waiting and watching myself
contemplate and analyze,
(I do love to over-analyze)
It is in those moments
where I see the way the words
seep from beneath my pores,
how they race to be heard,
even when I'm lost in them,

lost in the moment...

That is where I like to go,
like to hover,
a little outside the mind,
hiding undiscovered

(I lose myself to find myself)

We are
the restless ones,
the mad ones,
the reckless ones
with fractured hearts
We are the
the old souls found
in the lyrics of songs
We are the ones
people write into poems

(we were born for bigger things)

Ashley Jane

We watched the day change into night,
bright sunsets creating pink tourmaline skies,
caught up in the rise and fall
as we listened to the ocean's call

In that moment, nothing mattered
We forgot about everything wrong,
letting summer fade into autumn
as the ocean swallowed the sun

(serenity at sunset)

We were midnight songs
under the moon,
bodies lit up by the starlight
We spoke in sweet words and whispered oaths,
made pacts to meet here again
when life became too much
and we needed to escape

I think perhaps, I'm the only one that returned,
and my heart misses you more because of it

But, I'm proud of you,
the way you embraced the sun
Just promise, you'll remember where to go
if the dark starts calling your name

(I'll be waiting)

Dreams rise

as stars shine
against soft skies,

and we rest quietly,
enchanted by the sky above
and the waves that crash below

(night is always enchanting)

moonglade memories,
loose moments collected like change,
stored and saved up for a rainy day
when the clouds are dark
and a storm is settling somewhere in your soul

those little things that make hearts whole

(I keep them in a jar by the bed)

Ashley Jane

The sunlight shimmers,
watching us as it rises higher,
an artist painting the sky in shades of pink

The stars are faded,
and the moon is asleep

We follow a twisting path of poetry,
collecting driftwords
as they crash against the shore

We set fire to the shadows
until there are no more

(some days, we are the lightbringers)

We are dreams
that spill from treetops
and disappear at sunrise,
distant memories held safe
in a whirlwind of magic
and Milky Way madness

We spend the days
beneath a glaring sun,
waiting
impatiently
for the constellations
to awaken the wonder within,
to set our dreams free,
our hearts sleeping safe
in the arms of space

(dreaming of distant galaxies)

Whispers binding
you and me,
gently singing us to sleep
while under blankets of clouds,
we dream,
no longer separate entities

(the clouds know the best lullabies)

We are whispers
on paper
and screens
telling stories
about life
and desires
and heartache
to those who
speak the same language

(my language is letters and lines)

Some people
come into your life
knowing exactly what to say
and when to say it,
but some,
the very special ones,
never need to say anything at all

They shimmer,
their unbroken souls
so beautifully bold,
like vivid amber laced
with a cinnamon spark

They sing with ink and light my dark

(I keep them tethered to my heart)

Failing pulse
gently woken
with silent moments
painted in **VIVID** color

Our subconscious
becomes our savior

and dreams

rescue us,
revive us,
inspire us

restoring power
to our beating hearts

(we wake with bold souls)

I watched the waves,
lost in their rhythmic lull,
and I found a piece of myself

I stood under the stars,
captivated by their shine,
and I found a piece of myself

I looked in the mirror,
finally recognizing the face
that was staring back at me,
and I made peace with myself

(peace was my missing piece)

Love, Lies and Lullabies

Ashley Jane

So long ago,
I found myself in your poems,
kindred spirits with a thirst for more
You were magic and eloquence,
scrawling out stories of a heart softly shattered,
and I let every letter rain down around me

The years have passed,
but you'll still find me drifting through lines,
greedily devouring words
as well as spilling my own

(I've made poetry my home)

Love, Lies and Lullabies

Acknowledgements

To my other half who has had to listen to me talk about poems and poets and poetry on a daily basis, and who puts up with me pausing almost every television show because inspiration strikes. Thank you for putting up with my changing moods and the ongoing demands for silence. I love you.

To my family, my mom and my grandmother who have always supported me, even when they don't understand what I'm doing or why I need to do it. You've always encouraged me to pursue my dreams, so thank you. And to my grandfather and stepdad who have helped me so much along the way, I appreciate all you do. And to Jill, my other mother, I am so blessed to have you, and I am so grateful for everything. I love you all.

To Matt, my friend from the other side of the world. You've kept me sane in the crazy world of social media. Thank you so much for your friendship and your support, and another big thank you for proofreading and editing my book. You are awesome. I am so honored and blessed to know you.

To Alfa, I cannot thank you enough for your support and your faith in me. You have been such a blessing. Thank you for answering the million questions I asked without hesitation, for sharing your wisdom and pushing me to finish this book. I don't know where I'd be without you. Love ya!

To Chelsea, my wifey, thank you for always telling me I could do this and showing me what strength looks like. Love you.

To my UCC girls, thank you for being such a great group of friends, for always listening and being there, for making me laugh more times than I could ever count. You rock ladies!

To all the various readers and writers I've had the joy of getting to know. Thank you for all of the support and kind words and for encouraging me to write this book. You're all amazing.

To the various prompt hosts and feature pages, thank you for the inspiration and support. We are lucky to have a great poetry community.

Thank you to everyone who has bought this book of poetry. I hope you enjoy it.

About the Author

(written by M. Shirley)

For someone who professes to be somewhat anti-social, Ashley Jane is a person so inclusive and understanding of people, one could easily call her the socialite. Her acceptance of everyone she meets is, as her social media handle suggests, a breath of fresh air.

Poetess, studier of forensic psychology, and lupus survivor (though I consider her all but a lupus defeater), she lets nothing stop her love for the written word, and she is selfless in her inspiration of others; not only through social media circles however, but also within the criminal rehabilitation system. Her encouragement and support has helped many work through personal issues and addictions as they struggle to find their way in society.

A long time contributor of micro-poetry, she voluntarily runs a number of inspirational social media based prompts and writing pages to help others in their creative endeavors.

This, her first publication of poetry, brings together a small sample of her writing on Love, Lies and Lullabies in a reflective, accessible and thought provoking collection that many will relate to.

Ashley lives with her husband, extended family and a rather monkey like Shadow-cat, in Alabama, US...and it is from there that we feel and hear the whispers of her words that breath between night and day.

One could not ask for a more stalwart, loyal and supportive friend.

- seawords

Ashley Jane

Find Me on Social Media

Web: www.breathwords.com

Facebook: www.facebook.com/breathwords

Instagram: @breath_words_

Twitter: @breathwords

Pinterest: www.pinterest.com/breathwordspoems

Tumblr: @breathwords

Vero: @breathwords

You can also scan the QR code below:

www.ingramcontent.com/pod-product-compliance
Lightning Source LLC
Chambersburg PA
CBHW071204070526
44584CB00019B/2909